W9-BNQ-349

Using this book

Look at this book together. First talk about the pictures yourself, and point out things to look at. Let your child take her* time. With encouragement she will start to join in, talking about the familiar things in the pictures. Help her to count objects, to look for things that match, and to talk about what is going on in the picture stories.

*To avoid the clumsy use of he/she, the child is referred to as 'she'. The *Let's talk about* collection is suitable for both boys and girls.

Contents

A catalogue record for this book is available from the British Library

Published by Ladybird Books Ltd
27 Wrights Lane London W8 5TZ
A Penguin Company
2 4 6 8 10 9 7 5 3 1
Stories in this book were previously published by Ladybird Books Ltd.
in the *Toddler Talkabout* series.

My favourite things

Ladybird

I like
wild animals

Who can you see in the jungle?

How many animals can you count?

1 one

2 two

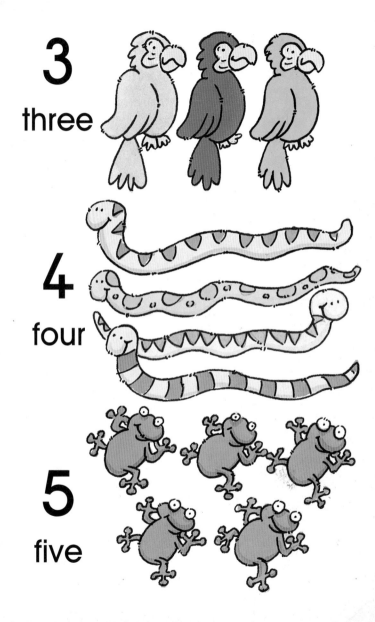

3 three

4 four

5 five

How many legs does the zebra have?

How many teeth does the hippo have?

What's happening here? Tell the story.

1

3

2

4

Find another…

zebra

lion

parrot

How many tigers are there
in the box?

How many now?

Poor Lion! Tell the story.

1

3

2

4

What baby animals can you see?

Who has furry skin and who has smooth skin?

Who's hiding in the jungle?

I like cars

Talk about these fast cars.

Do you like to go fast or slow?

What colours are these cars?

Which is your favourite colour?

This lady needs some petrol. Tell the story.

PETROL

OPEN

1

3

2

4

Point to the biggest car.

Do you like big cars or little cars?

How many cars are on the
transporter?

Look at the pictures and tell the story.

1

3

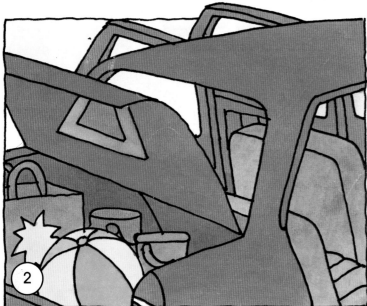

2

4

Who is stuck in this traffic jam?

How many red cars...

blue cars...

and yellow cars?

Now count the cars again.

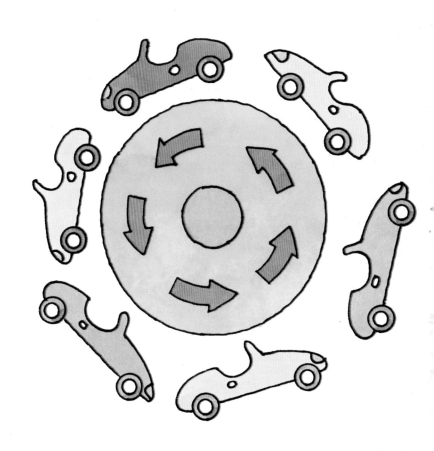

Which car do you like best?

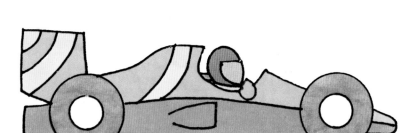

Are there any that you don't like?

What happens when the car breaks down?
Tell the story.

1

3

2

4

I like
farm animals

Who lives on the farm?

What animal noises can you make?

Moo!

Neigh!

Cock-a-doodle-doo!

Baa baa!

Cluck!

Quack quack!

What is happening in this story?

1

2

3

4

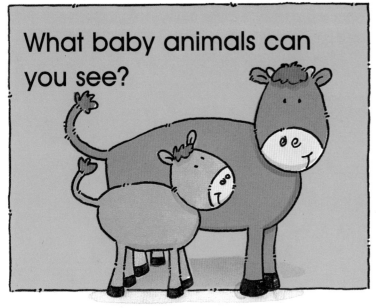

What baby animals can you see?

How many lambs can you count in each box?

Match these animals with their homes.

Can you match the animal to its blue shadow?

Say what is happening in
each box.

Find another...

cow

duck

horse

Which is your favourite farm animal?

What are the goats doing
in this story?

1

3

2

4

Sing 'Old Macdonald had a farm...'

I like
big trucks

Look for these big trucks when you go to town.

What colours are these trucks?

What is your favourite colour?

Count the dumper trucks.

How many red ones are there?

Look at the pictures and tell the story.

Point to the combine harvester.

What else can you see?

Look at the building site. Point to the cement mixer.

Match the drivers to their trucks.

Find another…

minibus

tanker

tractor

Which truck is the biggest? What jobs do you think they do?

Match each picture to its blue shadow.

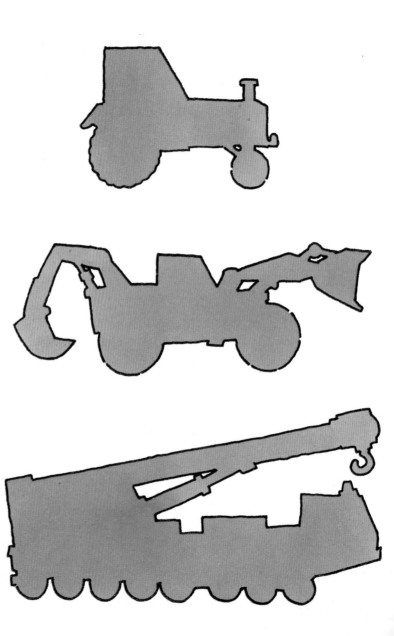

Count the lorries in each box.